PROBATE

A Guide for Real Estate Investors

Pierre Mouchette

Real Property Experts LLC
a Real Estate Knowledge Publication

Copyright © 2019 by Pierre Mouchette
All rights reserved. No part of this publication may be reproduced or used in any manner without written permission of the Copyright Holder, except by a reviewer who may quote brief passages in a review.

First Edition: December 2020
Real Property Experts LLC
Web Address: https://www.rpe4u.com
Contact: publications@rpe4u.com

Note: This publication comes in a variety of formats, such as Paperback Book | Print-on-Demand (POD) and Electronic Book (e-books). Some material included with the paperback versions of this book may not be included in e-books, and vice versa.

Disclaimer: This Real Property Experts LLC (RPE) publication provides information about the subject matter covered. The author and publisher of this content are not acting as licensed professionals in the presentation of covered material and are not qualified to give advice normally provided by professionals in the fields of expertise of this content, nor are they responsible for errors and omissions. The information and statements made, are for educational purposes and are not intended to replace a one-on-one relationship with a qualified attorney, accountant, tax professional, or other licensed professionals. You are solely responsible for the use of any content and hold Real Property Experts LLC, its' subsidiary's, and members harmless in any event or claim, demand, or damage, including reasonable attorneys' fees, asserted by any third party or arising out of your use of, or conduct on, articles and/or products.

RPE writers provide applicable content and break down complex topics so they are easier to understand. Information given may not apply to your specific situation, and products or services recommended may not be a good fit for your application. While RPE strives to provide accurate up-to-date content, we cannot guarantee the accuracy and completeness of information provided. By using this content, you understand that all material is an expression of opinions and not professional advice.

RPE regularly updates articles, but it is possible that we may miss something. Use our content as a starting point before selecting to use and choose a service or product. The reader is advised to keep up to date on activities in their locale by consulting with the appropriate licensed professionals for decisions that could affect them

PREFACE

What is Probate - this is a legal process in which a Will is reviewed to determine whether it is valid and authentic. Probate also refers to the general administering of a deceased person's Will or the estate of a deceased person without a Will. This Guide focuses on Real Estate owned by the decedent!

The Why - many beneficiaries do not want a property from a deceased relative. The reasons are many but can be whittled down to the following:

- The surviving spouse may not be able to keep up with the responsibilities of the home and wants to downsize.
- Younger heirs do not want to live in an older home, or it may be located too far from their employment.
- The recipient may not want the responsibility of investment property.
- The recipient may not be able to afford costs that coincide with the property.
- The recipient may need the cash generated from the property sale to pay-off current debts.

In any event that is where you as an investor come in! You can solve the above problems and turn the property into an opportunity.

For comments on this publication please write to us at REAL PROPERTY EXPERTS.

Pierre Mouchette, author
pierre@rpe4u.com

SPECIAL FEATURES

THE SYNCHRONICITY INVESTOR (**https://www.synchronicity-investor.com**) provides world class solutions for all. THE SYNCHRONICITY INVESTOR (TSI) is committed to providing you with the information that you need to make informed decisions. We encourage you to think of THE SYNCHRONICITY INVESTOR as your go to source for knowledgeable information. Additionally, on the website you can:

- Keep up to date – when there are important changes to our publications, we will post updates online.

- Publications – the website contains hundreds of articles on Real Estate, everyday Life, and the Environment, written by Pierre Mouchette and available for free. There you will find more Books, Booklets, How-to-Articles, Guides and much, much more.

Contents

EDUCATION ....- 6 -
CHAPTER 1 HAVING AN ESTATE ....- 7 -
   FINANCIAL IMPACT IN THE PREPARATION OF AN ESTATE ....- 8 -
CHAPTER 2 ESTATE PLANNING TOOLS ....- 13 -
   BASIC PROTECTION..- 14 -
   ESTATE PLANNING TOOLS TO MAXIMIZE YOUR ESTATE.................- 15 -
   ASSET PROTECTION TRUSTS ....- 17 -
   OF SPECIAL NOTE - THE INVESTOR ....- 18 -
CHAPTER 3 PROBATE ....- 20 -
   PROBATE COURT ....- 21 -
   PARTIES TO, AND THEIR FUNCTIONS IN THE PROBATE PROCESS- 22 -
   THE PROBATE PROCESS ....- 24 -
CHAPTER 4 THE REAL ESTATE INVESTOR ....- 31 -
   STATISTICS FOR 2019..- 32 -
   THE INVESTOR ....- 34 -
CHAPTER 5 PROBATE MARKETING ....- 37 -
   STARTING A PROBATE REAL ESTATE BUSINESS...............................- 41 -
   THE INSPECTION..- 46 -
   THE AGREEMENT ....- 48 -
   LETTER TO THE ESTATE EXECUTOR | ADMINISTRATOR ....- 50 -

EDUCATION

Through education, you find the entire process of probate to be lucrative. Real estate investors looking to find probate deals should take the time to familiarize themselves with the probate process and how it works. We recommend you start to learn this unique opportunity by planning an estate, specifically your own. In doing so, you will understand the how and why of the process while benefiting yourself and those you endear.

The following are items that are addressed within this guide:

- How to Find Probate Leads

- Marketing for Probate Properties

- Purchasing Probate Properties

- Selling Purchased Properties

- Building Your Professional Resume

CHAPTER 1   HAVING AN ESTATE

FINANCIAL IMPACT IN THE PREPARATION OF AN ESTATE

What Is Estate Planning?
Estate planning is the term given to the process people go through to prepare for the legal, financial, and personal realities of their death, while an estate plan is a collection of tools specifically designed to address these issues. Estate planning is not a single topic, but a collection of topics that all involve the practical realities surrounding death and mortality.

Planning can be complicated, in that it involves ever-changing considerations that involve personal preferences, new laws, shifting economic factors, and more. Regardless of your age or personal circumstances, creating an estate plan is an essential task for every adult, and understanding what an estate plan is and what specific kinds of issues your plan might address is the first step in planning.

What Is an Estate, and What Does Estate Planning Consist Of?
Many people confuse the term **'estate'** with the idea of a large home or property, but that is not what an estate is about. To understand, you must know the fundamentals such as:

- **Estate** - it is whatever a person leaves behind after death. Some people might leave a lot, while others might leave behind less. But everyone, no matter who they are, how much they own, or where they live, will leave behind an estate.

- **Estate Plans** - a collection of legally enforceable tools that allows individuals to control what happens to their estates after death. Some estate plans include a small number of tools (only a WILL, or a WILL with a testamentary trust), while others are more complicated.

- **Intestacy** - this is a state of denial in that some people are reluctant to think about death, and they never create an estate plan. People who die without leaving behind a plan are referred to as having died **'intestate.'** Because of this, all states have adopted laws that predetermines what happens to these estates. These laws are known as laws of intestacy, or intestate succession. Should you die without a will, your state's laws will automatically apply to your estate. Further, you have no control over what these laws choose, unless you override them with an estate plan of your own.

What is Probate?

Probate is the formal legal process that gives recognition to a Will and appoints the executor or personal representative who will administer the estate and distribute assets to the intended beneficiaries. The laws of each state vary, so it is a good idea to consult an attorney to determine whether a probate proceeding is necessary, whether the fiduciary must be bonded, and what reports must be prepared.

The basic job of administration and accounting for assets must be done whether the estate is handled by an **executor in probate or whether probate is avoided because all assets were transferred to a living trust during lifetime or jointly owned.** Many states have **'simplified or streamlined'** their probate processes over the years.

The probate process is intended to determine basic things, such as:

- Verifying the validity of the deceased person's will.

- Identify and inventory the deceased person's property.

- Have the property appraised and valued.

- Pay the deceased person's remaining debts and taxes.

- Distribute the deceased person's property to the appropriate people, entities, and / or charities.

Because everyone leaves behind an estate, all states have adopted laws that determine what happens to these items. While laws differ from state to state, they are basically the same, and allow for an efficient and uniform transfer of estate property to new owners. These are known as probate laws, or the probate code. Probate laws protect your right to make decisions about what you want to happen to your estate, but they also require you to make choices through specifically recognized methods, such as by making a **'last will and testament'** that complies with all applicable requirements.

What Are Some of The Basic Costs Related to Probate?

The cost of probate can include:

- Court fees.
- Attorney fees.
- Accounting and appraisal fees.

- Fees paid to the executor.

How expensive the probate process is, relates to the organization of the estate. If you must bring in accountants, attorneys, or other specialist to search for and evaluate the deceased person's assets, the fees can add up quickly. If the heirs of the estate contest the will and fight regarding the division of those assets, those costs can also increase the overall cost of the process.

The overall cost of probate can be 2 to 7-percent of the value of the estate, or more depending on the facts and circumstances of the individual case.

Are There Limitations to Executor and Probate Attorney Fees?
Fees paid to executors and probate attorneys are subject to state law, so these fees can vary by state. Depending on the amount of work that goes into administering the estate, these fees are often limited to about two to four percent of the estates' value.

Additional Probate Costs
In addition to the executor and attorney fees, there are court costs associated with the probate court. Court costs also vary from state to state, as well as with the type of estate and the paperwork that is required to be filed with the court.

Probate Planning, and Probate Avoidance
Probate laws can be complicated, cumbersome, and potentially expensive. Once you die and leave behind an estate, your inheritors cannot receive their inheritances until the probate process is completed.

For example, if the decedent left behind any debts, their creditors would have the opportunity to file a claim against the estate. Once filed, the executor (administrator) of the estate will have to use estate funds to pay off those debts before they can distribute any inheritances.

Today, many estate plans focus on taking probate out of the picture. There are many ways to do this.

For example, people who properly create and fund a 'living trust' can effectively make all (or all) of their major inheritance transfers completely outside of the probate process. Other probate mitigation tools can include providing lifetime gifts to friends and family, using payable-on-death assets such as life insurance policies, and taking advantage of jointly owned property.

Tax and Financial Planning

A good financial and estate plan can reduce the potential tax burden your estate might one-day face. In some situations, the right plan can allow you to avoid estate, and inheritance taxes completely. However, as with any discussion of tax issues, it is important to note that current tax laws can and will change in the future. This is one of the many reasons why talking to an **'estate planning expert'** will always be better than trying to craft a plan on your own.

Estate Taxes

Estate taxes, sometimes referred to as the **'death tax,'** are widely misunderstood by the general population. When you die and leave behind an estate, that estate is worth a certain dollar amount. An estate tax is simply a tax applied to that value.

The estate tax is a tax that you will never have to pay because it only applies after you die. Additionally, it is not a tax your family or inheritors will have to pay because your estate is responsible for paying it before distributing property as inheritances. If an estate is asset-rich but cash-poor, paying the estate tax may require the liquidation of some assets, to cover the estate tax bill. Furthermore, any time an estate must pay estate taxes, the tax paid reduces potential inheritances.

The Federal Government has an estate tax, but it does not currently apply unless you leave behind an estate worth more than $11.18 million dollar if you are single, or more than $22.36 million if you are married. If you leave an estate worth less than this amount, your estate will not have to pay any federal estate taxes.

In addition to the federal estate tax, some states have also enacted state-level estate taxes of their own. These state-level taxes can apply to much smaller estates. Crafting an estate plan that reduces or eliminates any potential state estate tax assessment can be vital if you want to preserve as many of your assets as possible to use for inheritances.

Inheritance Taxes
There is no federal inheritance tax, and only a small number of states currently have inheritance taxes. For 2019 there are currently six states with inheritance tax Iowa, Kentucky, Maryland, Nebraska, New Jersey, and Pennsylvania.

CHAPTER 2 ESTATE PLANNING TOOLS

BASIC PROTECTION

Last Will and Testament - this is the most well-known estate planning tool because people know and understand that by making one, they can choose what kinds of inheritances they leave behind. But making a **Will** is a lot more complicated than just writing your wishes down on a piece of paper. Every state has specific rules that apply to people who make a Will, and if you fail to follow those rules, your Will is useless. These requirements include:

- Being at least 18 years old.
- Being of sound mind.
- Making your will in writing.
- Signing the document.
- Having the document signed by two competent adult witnesses.

Nevertheless, meeting the basic legal requirements is not enough to ensure your will does what you want it to do. An effective will is one that not only meets state requirements, but also one that is matched to your needs and desires.

- **Transfer-on-Death Assets** - also known as **'payable-on-death'** this asset is an estate planning and inheritance tool. This asset is a life insurance policy, that is automatically inherited by your chosen beneficiary following your demise. With this tool you do not need to make a will or a trust to choose who inherits the asset. You simply need to make sure you choose your beneficiary in the manner required under the asset's rules.

- **Medical Power of Attorney** - anyone can become incapacitated as the result of a medical emergency, with this becoming a tragedy when no plan of continuation exists. A durable medical power of attorney can let you control who will make your medical decisions if you are unable.

- **Financial Power of Attorney** - as an investor, you want to grant financial power of attorney to a trusted individual. Rents must be collected, tenants or management handled, and payments must be made if your business is to survive in your absence. Financial power of attorney grants these powers and can be created independently or alongside medical power of attorney.

ESTATE PLANNING TOOLS TO MAXIMIZE YOUR ESTATE

These tools will help protect you and your assets from creditors, minimize federal and state estate tax, and maximize income tax opportunities available to you.

Estate Planning Trusts

These are popular estate planning tools, and one of the least understood. A trust is like a small corporation in that it exists as a legal entity apart from the person who creates it. Trusts can own property like a corporation and are run by people who do not own the property, but who simply manage it or look after it on the trust's behalf. While there are numerous kinds of trusts you can include in your estate plan, one of the main benefits of using a trust is as an inheritance vehicle. **Unlike wills, trust's do not have to go through the probate process.**

- **Revocable Living Trust** (also known as an inter-vivo trust) - allows you to make inheritance choices without submitting those choices to a probate court. To avoid probate, you can put all your assets into a revocable living trust. This written document (signed and notarized) determines who will receive the property when you die. To do this, you must create a trust document and then transfer any assets into that trust. Typically, the revocable living trust is the **'mothership'** containing many sub-trusts.

- **Irrevocable Living Trust** - are contracts created to transfer or manage assets of an individual that the trust creator claims are not competent to manage property or other assets. The irrevocable aspect can be limited to a portion of the trust, so other parts of the trust could be changed. Depending on the terms of these trusts, they cannot be changed or reversed.

- **Qualified Personal Residence Trust** - a specific type of trust that allows its creator to remove a personal home from his or her estate for the purpose of reducing the amount of gift tax that is incurred when transferring assets to a beneficiary. Definition from (www.investopedia.com/terms/q/qualified-personal-residence-trust.asp)

- **Granter Retained Annuity Trust** - an irrevocable trust that is used when a portion of the trust assets are to be paid out to the settler during a pre-defined period. At the end of the term, the trust assets are distributed to the beneficiaries and gift taxes are avoided.

- **Testamentary Trust** - a trust set up by the terms of a person's will, which goes into effect upon their death. This form of trust does not avoid the probate process since the trust was not funded during the settler's lifetime and the assets were still under the direct control of the settlor at the time of death.

- **Irrevocable Life Insurance Trust** - used to exclude life insurance proceeds from the decedent's estate. It is often employed in conjunction with other trusts and estate planning tools. This type of trust can provide a source of assets which can be utilized by the beneficiaries to pay estate taxes or other expenses associated with settling the estate, eliminating the need to access the decedent's other trusts.

ASSET PROTECTION TRUSTS

- **Domestic Asset Protection Trust (DAPT)** - created in states that have anti-creditor trust acts (Alaska, Delaware, South Dakota, Nevada, and some others), and allows an individual to establish a trust for his or her own assets that offers protection from creditors.

- **Offshore Asset Protection Trust** - this is considered the strongest asset protection strategy available, with this trust being established in a non-domestic jurisdiction and allowing assets to be conveyed to offshore trusts for protection from seizure in judgments for creditors.

- **Totten Trust** - this trust allows an individual to put money into a bank account or other form of security to be held until death, when the contents of the account will pass to a designated beneficiary without having to deal with probate. This is also known as a pay on death designation.

- **IRA Trust** - to preserve assets from taxation, an individual can establish a trust as the beneficiary of an IRA account, which protects the beneficiaries, such as young children or adult children with special needs.

OF SPECIAL NOTE - THE INVESTOR

Estate planning for real estate investors is unlike that of others. Why? .... investors are a different breed of people, who have unique concerns throughout their lives and then beyond.

If you have ever wondered about what will become of your real estate assets at the end of your life, you need to think about **Succession Planning** for your business and of course transferring those assets to beneficiaries without paying unnecessary expenses.

- **The Living Trust and Pour-Over Will** - for the real estate investor who buys and sells assets frequently, it is important to know that you should update your estate plan each time you make a substantial purchase or sale. This could present a challenge for an active investor with many properties, but the problem can be easily addressed by using a **'pour-over will.'**

    For the real estate investor, a **'pour-over will pairs well with a living trust,'** as this type of will passes all property you own to said living trust upon your death. This ensures a smooth, private transition of your assets. As such, using these tools together is a smart tactic for a clear, easy-to-follow business succession plan that you direct.

A Final Word
Estate Planning and Probate is a complicated task and must be done in accordance with your wishes, subject to your state's laws. Use the professional services provided by an estate attorney for compliance!

CHAPTER 3   PROBATE

PROBATE COURT

Probate Courts have jurisdiction over the administration and oversight of trusts and estates. These matters account for most of the courts' work and include the following:

- Probating wills and the administration of estates.
- Overseeing testamentary and living trusts.
- Determining title to real and personal property.
- Construing the meaning of wills and trusts.

What Is Probate?
Probate is a legal term that refers to the process of distributing the estate of a deceased person according to their Will. To avoid conflict and future legal action. The estate needs to be executed according to the Will of the deceased. For an asset to be transferred from the deceased to the person they chose, the Will must go through the probate process.

This process will not only ensure that the estate is distributed according to the decedents Will but, will also ensure that all debts and taxes are settled before the estate is transferred to those named in the Will. The Will usually names an Executor, who in most cases, is a trusted family member or friend. The Executor will ensure that the decedents Will is executed according to his or her wish.

What If There is No Will?
In many cases, if there is no Will, or if some of the estate's assets have no designated beneficiary, there is a court-supervised process that distributes the assets. This same probate process allows a challenging of the Will, where the court will decide who the beneficiary will be.

PARTIES TO, AND THEIR FUNCTIONS IN THE PROBATE PROCESS

Estate Administrator - the person or entity named by the Probate Court to perform the duties normally fulfilled by the Executor of the Estate. This appointment is due to the decedent not having a Will, or if the executor listed in a Will is deemed incapable by a court.
The Estate Administrator is also known as **a 'personal representative of the estate.'**

Probate Attorney - also called Estate or Trust Attorneys, help Executors of the Estate (or Estate Administrators, if there is no Will) manage the probate process. **They also help with estate planning, such as the drafting of Wills or Trusts; advise on Powers of Attorney; or even serve as an Executor or Estate Administrator.**

Executor - the manager of the decedents' property. In some states, if the executor is female, they are called an executrix. Other states simply use the term personal representative or administrator.

Fiduciary - a person who holds a legal or ethical relationship of trust with one or more parties.

Probate Judge - a Probate Judge is a Civil Court Judge and a state judicial official who oversees all aspects of the **'probate court system.'** Estate matters are the most common cases heard in probate courts.

Not all states and counties have probate courts, and in some, they are called Surrogate's Courts. By either name, they cover the same legal issues and the judges assigned to them share the same roles and in some, they are called Surrogate's Courts. By either name, they cover the same legal issues and the judges assigned to them share the same roles and responsibilities.

Hiring a Probate Attorney - With a Will

The probate process will go smoother when the decedent has drafted a Will prior to their demise. If a person dies with a Will, a probate attorney may be hired to advise parties such as the executor of the estate or a beneficiary on various legal matters

There are numerous reasons that Wills may be challenged, although most Wills go through probate without a problem. Additionally, a probate attorney may be responsible for performing any of the following tasks when advising an executor:

- Collecting and managing life insurance proceeds.
- Getting the decedent's property appraised.
- Finding and securing all the decedent's assets.
- Advising on how to pay the decedent's bills and settle debts.
- Preparing / filing documents as required by probate court.
- Managing the estate's checkbook.
- Determining whether any estate taxes are owed.

Hiring a Probate Attorney - Without a Will

If you die without having a written and signed Will, you are said to have died intestate. When this happens, your estate is distributed according to the intestacy laws of the state where the property resides, regardless of your wishes. In these situations, a probate attorney may be hired to assist the administrator of the estate (like the executor) and the assets will be distributed according to state law. A probate attorney may help with some of the tasks listed above but is bound by state intestacy laws, regardless of the decedent's wishes or the family members' needs.

A relative who wants to be the estate's administrator must first secure what are called **'renunciations'** from the decedent's other relatives. A renunciation is a legal statement renouncing ones right to administer the estate. A probate attorney can help secure and file these statements with the probate court, and then assist the administrator with the probate process (managing the estate checkbook, determining estate taxes, securing assets, etc.).

THE PROBATE PROCESS

The probate process may seem confusing because of the proceedings involved, and the execution of state mandated laws. This guide will briefly explain procedures so that you will be aware of and understand how as an investor you can help all parties involved in the probate process. Always remember that probate is not a one two three process, it can take from three months two several years to complete, depending on the complexity of the estate, family relations, and directions left by the decedent.

The Petition

A petition for **'Petition or Probate of Will,'** should be submitted to the **Probate Court** within 30 days of the decedent's death. It should be accompanied by the original **Will and Codicils,** if any, and a **certified copy of the death certificate.** The petition must also contain the names and addresses of all heirs, beneficiaries and interested parties with verification that each has been notified of the **Petition for Administration or Probate of Will** received by them by mail.

The hearing on the petition may be held in probate court and is an opportunity for family members and other interested parties to ask questions or state their positions. For the hearing these are the following options:

- The court may send notice to all parties informing them of the time and place of the hearing. If written waivers are filed by those receiving the notice, and the court does not believe a hearing is necessary, the court may enter a decree without a formal hearing and without the parties being present.

- The court may follow the **'streamline'** notice procedure, where the court notifies all parties that they have the right to a hearing if requested by a specified date. If a party requests a hearing, the court will send notice and hold a hearing. If no hearing is requested, the court may, without the presence of the parties, issue a decree on the decree entry date specified in the notice.

The result is that the court will formally appoint the Executor named in the Will when the Will is admitted to probate. If the estate is intestate, the court will appoint an Administrator. Be aware that the court requires that the administrator provide a probate bond. However, the court may dispense with the requirement of a bond if:

- The Will excuses the bond.
- The assets of the estate are less than the state mandated amount.
- All heirs or beneficiaries waive the requirement of a bond.

The court then gives the Executor legal documents **called Letters Testamentary or Letters of Administration.** These documents authorize the Executor to distribute assets to beneficiaries. This may include transferring assets from the decedent's name into the names of the beneficiaries and paying any debts or taxes on behalf of the estate.

If the descendent owned property in more than one state, it may be necessary to conduct additional Probate proceedings in those states where the other properties are located. This may require the executor to hire an attorney in both the state of primary residence and the state or states where the additional property is located.

Administration

For the probate process to begin, the Executor must inventory the assets of the estate, and file an inventory of the estate with the Probate Court within the state specified time. In general, the inventory should list any property the decedent owned in their name, including real estate, bank accounts, stocks and bonds, motor vehicles, household furnishings and personal effects. It should include life insurance policies only if payable to the decedent's estate. Partnership property and any property owned with other persons not in survivorship.

The inventory should not include property held in such a way that it passes outside of probate, such as by joint survivorship or beneficiary designation or property held in a trust.

After giving the inventory to the court, the fiduciary should open an estate account and then transfer all bank accounts from the decedent's name into the estate account. The Executor will need a certified copy of their appointment as Executor from the Probate Court and a Tax ID Number to do this. Additionally, all transfer agents should be notified and instructed to send dividends in care of the Executor. Utility companies need to be notified of the decedent's death and accounts that will remain open should be transferred to the estate. All real property should be secured, protected from the elements, and insured under the estate.

Valuation

All property must be valued on the inventory list at its fair market value at the time of death. It is the responsibility of the Executor to determine these values through inquiry and at their own experience. The value of real estate may be determined in one of several ways, including:

- A written appraisal.
- A comparative market analysis by a real estate agent.

Itemized lists of valuable personal property, such as jewelry and antiques, should also be included. Household furnishings and personal items need not be itemized unless of certain (probate court determined) value.

The Executor must send copies of the inventory lo each party and attorney involved with the estate and must certify on the inventory that copies have been provided to same.

Listing Real Property:

- **Property Appraisal** - if the property is to be sold, the Executor will then determine a listing price for the property in question. The listing price will be determined after an appraisal with the help of a real estate agent experienced in probate sales.

- **Property Listing** - after the listing price is established, the property will then be put on the market. The real estate agent working with the property will market it like any other home, using signage, websites, and more to attract the highest offer.

- **Approval and Sale** - once an offer is submitted, the real estate agent will negotiate the terms to satisfy all parties. If there are no objections, a court date will be scheduled where the sale of the house will be officially executed.

Selling to An Investor:

- **Property Appraisal** - if the property is to be sold, the Executor will then determine the asking price based on the appraisal.

- **Investor** - the Executor can contact investors in the area and ask them to submit a **'cash bid'** for the property.

- **Approval and Sale** - once offers are submitted, the Executor will negotiate a final price with the bidders to satisfy both parties. An official notice will be mailed to all heirs of the estate, establishing a specific day period to object to the sale of the property. If there are no objections, a court date will be scheduled where the sale of the house will be officially executed.

Estate Administration Expenses

The Executor should anticipate the cash needs of the estate to pay for administration expenses, taxes, claims and bequests. As a fiduciary they have the authority to convert into cash any personal property not specifically bequeathed but must obtain permission from the Probate Court to sell, mortgage or otherwise convey real estate, unless specifically authorized to do so under the terms of the Will.

When personal property is to be sold, the fiduciary (if the fiduciary is not named in the Will as executor or is not a family member) must send a copy of the inventory to all interested parties, with a notice of intent to sell. The parties have the right to object to the sale within a time determined by the court or, the court may waive this requirement if an expeditious sale is necessary. If parties interested in the estate do not want certain assets sold, cash may be advanced to the estate to pay estate obligations.

The surviving spouse or other dependent family members may apply to the Probate Court for a support allowance from the estate during the period of settlement of the estate. The court may allow the surviving spouse or family of the decedent to use the decedent's automobile while the estate is being settled, provided the decedent maintained the automobile as a family car.

Claims Against the Decedent

Claims refer to debts incurred during the decedent's lifetime and unpaid at the time of death. It is the fiduciary's responsibility to determine the validity of any claims presented.

After the Executor's appointment, the Probate Court will place a newspaper notice informing the estate's creditor of the decedent's death, the creditors' obligations to present their claims promptly, the Executor's name and the address where claims are to be presented. Creditors have a state mandated time (usually within 150 days), to present their claims to the Executor. The Executor must determine the legal validity of each claim and notify the creditor whether the claim is allowed or rejected, in whole or in part. If there is doubt regarding the validity of a claim, the Executor should seek legal assistance.

The estate will also be responsible for paying some expenses that arise after the decedent's death. Funeral expenses take priority over all other expenses for which the estate is responsible. Administration expenses include statutory probate fees, attorney's fees, fiduciary's fees, the cost of legal notices and any expenses related to maintenance of the decedent's property incurred after the decedent's death. If the estate is insufficient to pay all proper expenses, some of them will take precedence over others. Before paying claims and expenses, the Executor should consult with their Probate Attorney to ascertain the priority of claims to be paid.

> *If the assets of the estate are not adequate to pay the debts, the estate may be settled as insolvent. The fiduciary should obtain competent advice from their Probate Attorney.*

File Tax Returns and Pay Applicable Taxes
Yes, taxes are still payable as a result of death and include the federal estate tax, state estate tax, and gift tax. Both estate taxes have provisions that exempt estates below established thresholds from taxation. Taxes may also be payable to other states in which the decedent owned property. In addition, a decedent may owe other taxes, such as income taxes and property taxes. The Executor is responsible for filing necessary tax returns and paying taxes in connection with the estate. Executors must also report income received during estate administration.

File Final Financial Report or Account
Every Executor must file a financial report or account with the court when the administration of the estate is complete or when the Executor seeks to resign or is removed by the court.

The Executor must provide copies of the financial report or account to each party and attorney involved with the estate and must certify on the document that the copies have been provided.

The Probate Court will hold a hearing on the financial report or account to allow the beneficiaries or any other interested party to ask questions about, or object to, the way estate funds were managed.

Distribute Assets to Beneficiaries

A final financial report or account must report all distributions made to heirs or beneficiaries as well as distributions that are proposed to be made. When the court approves the final financial report or account, it will order the Executor to distribute the remaining assets of the estate according to the approved distribution.

- **Closing** - the final accounting is filed with the court, outlining all financial steps taken during the administration phase (actions taken, and debts paid). Remaining funds are then used to pay attorney and court fees, with the balance remaining distributed to beneficiaries.

Once the debts are paid and the tangible property is distributed, the appointee can move to the closing phase.

What Happens to The Personal Belongings Inside the House?

Due to the monetary and sentimental value of an estate, probate is designed to prevent the Executor from making hasty, emotional decisions. In a probate scenario, nothing should happen to the home (or the contents in it) upon the death of the homeowner, and the home should remain physically untouched until an executor is named.

Once the executor is named, he or she can take inventory and have the assets appraised, including the home's contents and its market value. Personal belongings in the property will be distributed among the heirs or the personal property will be sold off in an estate sale prior to the closing of the home.

There are two paths for a house in probate: Conveyance to survivors, or a probate home sale. Ultimately, what happens to a home in probate varies from state-to-state but generally one of two things will happen:

1) Beneficiaries of the estate will inherit the property, or

2) The house will need to be sold through probate court.

In all cases:

- Death does not release a mortgage. Those who inherit the property will assume the monthly payments.

- Beneficiaries may be responsible for capital gains tax if the home in probate goes up in value. The faster the home can get to market, the better.

- Homes can be titled so beneficiaries or co-granter can inherit your home automatically upon death.

Does the Will Give Authority to Sell Property?
Once the decedent's Will is authenticated by the probate court, if the Will authorizes the sale of real or personal property, the Executor | Administrator need not seek court approval for the sale, for any reason without limitation if it is in the best interest of the estate. If the Will places limitations on the power of sale, those limitations will remain in effect.

If the Will has not authorized the sale of the estate property, they may still do so by getting the permission of the probate court. If the Executor | Administrator is required to sell personal property of the estate and fails to do so, keeping, using, or transferring it for their own benefit, they could be held personally liable.

Can A House Be Sold While in Probate?
Absolutely! You will need to be the Executor | Administrator of the estate and obtain permission from the other heirs. The money received will go towards the estate's debts, and then divided between the beneficiaries. The sale must be approved by the heirs and the court to move forward in the process.

When going through the probate process, the faster you can sell the home, the less stressful the whole situation will become. A direct cash offer from an investor can be completed much quicker rather than going through the steps of probate. By going through a Probate Real Estate Investor, you can save your family time, money, and a lot of unnecessary stress. Probate circumstances are stressful and can lead to heated arguments amongst family members that can tear a family apart.

CHAPTER 4   THE REAL ESTATE INVESTOR

STATISTICS FOR 2019

Real estate statistics give investors data-based insight into the constantly shifting housing market. This can be helpful when setting buying expectations, finding the right property, and negotiating the right price. For the most accurate look at the current real estate market, review the statistics below:

People under 35 years old make up 35% of homeowners.
This demographic includes newly married couples and people with young children. These buyers are seeking starter homes or new constructions to fit into their budget. *Source: U.S. Census Bureau, 2019*

More than 78% of homeowner are 65 years old or older.
While this number has decreased over the past 20 years, this means that a large portion of sellers of pre-existing homes are of retirement age, seeking to downsize. *Source: U.S. Census Bureau, 2019*

The median price of a home in the U.S. in 2019 is $277,000.
Median prices increase and decrease nationwide each month. Given the average cost of starter homes in the U.S. (just over $219,000, according to NAR), this indicates developers are targeting homebuyers seeking homes in lower price tiers. *Source: National Association of Realtors, 2019*

Only 28% of homebuyers found a home using an agent.
Many buyers believe that the most common way to find a house is using a real estate agent. The reality is that-according to NAR, most people find a new home online and then locate an agent to show them the property. *Source: National Association of Realtors, 2018*

Homes that are staged sell 25% faster.
Staging gives buyers the ability to see how a room is designed and visualize themselves living in the home. However, many agents use virtual staging to increase sale ability while avoiding the cost of physical staging. *Source: Coldwell Banker, 2019*

Only 8% of homeowners regret buying instead of renting.
According to Zillow, only 8% of homeowners regret buying a property. Of the regrets for buying a property, unexpected maintenance costs and being locked into one location are the top concerns. *Source: Zillow, 2019*

Americans spend, on average, 50% of their earnings on buying a home.
This includes the initial down payment, but more significantly, regular mortgage payments and upkeep costs. *Source: PWC Emerging Trends in Real Estate, 2019*

Married people make up 63% of all homeowners.
Many people who get married consider buying a home. This means that the other 37% are divorced, separated, or single. For agents, it appears that the best target demographic for new clients is married (or soon-to-be-married) couples. *Source: NAR Home Buyers and Sellers Generational Trends Report, 2019*

THE INVESTOR

What is a Probate Real Estate Investor?
This is an Investor who specializes in working with Attorneys, Executors / Administrators, and Family Members of deceased owner properties. The Investor helps parties to the property in probate by making an offer to purchase.

Benefits of Purchasing Probate Properties
The main reason that this niche investment opportunity has not been exploited is that the process is slow and requires a lot of patience. Probate properties sell below market value more than any other property type. Investing in probate real estate properties offers many benefits such as:

- **Motivated Sellers** - sellers of probate properties are motivated to sell the home quickly. Whether it is the estate or the heirs, the seller most likely wants the property to sell as effortlessly as possible. Many owners live out of state and do not have the time, energy, or money to maintain the property. If the Investor is buying the property with cash, they should share that information with the seller.

- **High Percentage of Clear Titles** - a high percentage of properties in probate do not have a mortgage. Buying investment properties for cash without any liens, is a great way to make money.

- **Properties Priced Below Market Value** - because of the nature of probate properties, the price is often competitive and below market value. The heirs may prefer to receive the cash instead of the responsibility of the property. Also, the seller might not want to have to conduct repairs before they sell the property, making the price more attractive instead.

- **Low Competition** - the competition with probate properties is low. Many real estate investors do not understand or are not aware of probate properties. This works to your advantage due to low competition.

Investor Qualifications

To perform the work function, the Investor must have:

- General real-estate transaction experience.
- Real estate probate knowledge.
- A working knowledge of federal, state, and local laws regarding real estate and probate.
- Excellent interpersonal communications.
- Good planning skills.
- Good marketing skills and techniques.
- Knowledge in market research and property analysis.
- Knowledge of market values.
- The ability to prepare a comparable market analysis.
- Estimates of repair cost.
- The ability to spend time with the attorney, executor, or administrator of the estate.
- Means to provide earnest money deposit.
- Be pre-approved for a mortgage loan, or better (funds to purchase and close).

What Other Options Does the Investor Provide?

The Investor wants their inventory to sell fast and provide them with cash flow. They will:

- Sell to another investor.
- Sell the property with owner financing.
- Provide lease options or rent to own options.
- Rent the property.

Goals for The Investor

Set Investment Goals - setting clear and specific investment goals is the road map, and course of action to being successful. You are statistically more likely to achieve goals by writing them down in a business plan and setting dates to accomplish the goal by.

Continuing Education - without knowledge you cannot continue to succeed. Knowledge will take you up the ladder of success as a plausible investor to a prodigious investor.

The Probate Real Estate Purchase Process

You can purchase real estate that is in probate either through an auction or from a direct sale. Although there are differences between the two processes, many of the same requirements exist, no matter which procedure is deployed. If you are awarded the sale, you must have an order from the probate court that approves the sale. The attorney, executor or administrator of the estate is responsible for obtaining the order approving the sale from the court. You cannot finalize the sale without the court's approval.

Once the order approving the sale is issued by the court, the attorney for the estate will prepare a deed transferring ownership of the real estate to you. The deed becomes legally effective when it is filed with the register of deeds in the county where the real estate is located.

- **Auction** - you can attend the auction scheduled by the executor or administrator of the estate and bid on the property. If you are the highest bid, you have obligated yourself to making the purchase. You must then provide the estate with a certified check to cover the price you bid on the real estate. Typically, this check represents proceeds from a loan already approved by a lender. In lieu of a certified check, you must provide proof of preapproval for a loan that covers the price you bid on the real estate (if previously agreed to by the estate).

- **Direct Sale** - the process of purchasing real estate through probate or trust is a series of court-regulated steps that must be carefully monitored and managed. Deadlines are unforgiving, documentation is specialized, and the court's oversight must be honored throughout the marketing, offers, negotiations and sale of the property.

Make a direct offer on the real estate to the attorney, executor or administrator of the estate. If the estate's representative accepts your offer, they will present the offer to the probate court.

CHAPTER 5   PROBATE MARKETING

Your brand is the heart of your business. As part of your real estate brand identity, a successful marketing campaign has the power to build trust and dismantle fears that customers may have. An effective real estate marketing campaign is a crucial component to separating your business from the pack.

Marketing

A well-organized marketing campaign encompasses a combination of factors to create, communicate, deliver, and exchange an investor's message to consumers, but its core functions are to do one thing, generate leads. Specifically, leads on deceased owner properties. As a professional investor in this **'niche market'** your experience and reputation will precede you with those involved in probate.

Since marketing is used to attract people, it is one of the primary components of business management and commerce. As a marketer you can direct your campaigns to other businesses (B2B marketing) or directly to consumers (B2C marketing).

Now that these factors have been established, you must decide on the methodology of deploying your services to market the product (i.e., your business and the properties you obtain).

Probate Leads

You can find leads for your business by searching through:

- Court Records.
- Networking with Estate Planning and Probate Attorneys.
- Newspapers Obituaries.
- Probate Courts.
- The Internet.

A good probate list will include property information such as ownership status, mortgage information (when applicable) and most importantly, the contact information for those who may be involved with the potential sale of the property.

Often a deceased person's executor/administrator will run a notice in the local newspaper to give creditors and potential heirs a chance to come forward and stake a claim to any property. This is another way to quickly find probate leads and contact information.

Marketing for Probate Listings

Handing the processes of probate are businesses that are in the business of serving those in that genre. For marketing purposes, we will concentrate on those that you can create a direct mail marketing campaign for.

Content that you generate should be tailor-made for those in control of probate - properties. That is, Business to Business (B2B) and Business to Consumer (B2C) with you as the business in both cases.

The content of the program should be as follows:

B2B (Business to Business) - this can be a form letter to businesses

- **Estate Attorneys** - they provide counsel and help in the planning of Living Wills, Wills, and Trusts for their clients. The attorney additionally helps their clients determine the specific distribution of their estate for future beneficiaries. Drafting Wills, Trusts and other estate planning documents is a significant part of their job.

- **Probate Lists** - as the name states a probate list is just that, a list of all the homes in probate within that court's jurisdiction. These lists are available from specialized publishers, the local courthouse, and probate court. While these lists are convenient, they may contain slightly older probates or even inherited properties.

- **Real Estate Firms** - this is a difficult chore to accomplish unless you personally know of a real estate agent who can lead you in the right direction; have access to the Multiple Listing Service (MLS); or go to probate court and ask the clerk where you can obtain the information, or to point you in the right direction.

- **Google it** - use your computer to do the search for you. Enter: Probate Court - {city, state} Real Estate & Homes for Sale; {state} Probate Real Estate Sales; and be creative with other verbiage.

B2C (Executors/Administrators and Family Members) - handwritten professionally composed letter and handwritten envelope. Given the nature of your campaign, you may find the most success with these personalized handwritten letters. They will also portray your sincerity, and not come across as spammy.

If you receive no response from your initial letter, follow up with a second and third letter on a three then four-week basis. You should never send more than three letters!

All letters generated **MUST** incorporate the following:

- Compassion.
- Appeal to the needs of the executor or heir.
- Offer a compassionate service such as offering to pay for professional clean-out services.

STARTING A PROBATE REAL ESTATE BUSINESS

As an entrepreneur, businessperson and professional, you must advertise to let potential customers and attorneys, executors and administrators recognize your name (brand identification), know what you do, and how to reach you.

Let the seller know that your company purchases properties fast at a reasonable investor discount, and that you can help save them undue duress. They should know:

- Real-estate agent commissions can amount to thousands of dollars.

- Homes sold by agents must be prepared for sale (cost the seller's money).

- You do not require showings, which will take up their time, and be a constant source of their privacy being invaded.

- You purchase houses in as-is condition.

- You can give them a purchase price and close quickly, thereby saving them from the real-estate agent negotiation process, which can typically take days or weeks, as offers and counteroffers are communicated back and forth.

- You can put a house under contract within twenty-four to forty-eight hours, reducing their stress.

- Selling to the average buyer requires them to apply for a mortgage and before they are approved, a month or more can go by and then they are not approved. Then the whole process starts over! A waste of time when you can pay cash.

That your company focuses on solutions where everyone wins. You are the option for families who need to sell and move fast.

Advertising

An important part of being a real estate investor is advertising! Having qualified leads is what it is all about! If you have no leads you have no deals, and without deals you will make absolutely nothing.

- **Business Cards** - (this miniature billboard is the cheapest way for you to introduce yourself to potential leads). Every time you talk with someone about your real estate business give them three cards. Why three? They will be able to hand the other two to an associate or friend. This will grow your business by word of mouth!

- **Direct Mail** - direct mail campaigns work! You can obtain your leads from the courthouse, local paper, list service providers, MLS, probate court and more.

Marketing

In most markets across the country, there are plenty of eager Investors ready to purchase a property in cash so long as there is a profit to be made. Therefore, most experienced investors are more interested in finding properties that can be quickly flipped.

When you have a deal locked up and under contract that offers a salacious profit margin, it will not be difficult to find a buyer and make a sale happen. In most markets, ravenous cash buyers are plentiful.

It is also worth noting that legit investors can close on the sale of a property in a matter of days. This is largely because he or she is paying in cash. In a market filled with competing investors, he or she does not want to risk missing an opportunity.

There are many benefits to being able to zero in on EXACTLY what your buyers want:

- You can stretch your marketing dollars and efforts much further by zeroing in on the most in-demand areas, and properties ignoring the rest.

- You will have buyers already lined up to strike if you can bring them the right deal.

- You will have a much easier time knowing when a deal is a deal as it hits your desk.

- You will not risk under-bidding or over-bidding on a deal and losing it.

- You will know exactly what to offer, since you know what buyers are willing to pay.

- Overall, you will work less and make more.

Whatever you decide, at the end of the day your investing business will be dead unless you build a steady, reliable pipeline of motivated seller leads into your business. This pipeline will be the source of all your profits.

Once you implement your marketing plan, the idea is to start getting motivated sellers ringing your phone off the hook on a regular basis. This is no easy matter and will take work, especially considering that you will need to speak with as many as 30 to 40 sellers before you get a deal under contract. So, the question is, how do you get the phone to ring in the first place?

Most lead-generation strategies can be broken down into three categories:

- Off-line Lead Generation Methods.
- On-line Lead Generation Methods.
- Hybrid of the two methods.

A successful investing business that has achieved scale will ideally employ all the above, though it can be quite common to see a business depend on only one type of lead generation, which it has perfected and optimized.

Communicating with Executors | Administrators

Probate leads are one of their best lead sources, there are still many real estate investors who are reluctant to get started in this business. One common concern is that they are unsure of how to communicate with the estates Executor or Administrator.

- **Determine Your Contact Strategy** - using a formal letter as your initial point of contact, followed by similar letters or postcards every other month. The letter should be sympathetic. The reader has most likely lost a loved one and is in the middle of a difficult time in his/her life. We recommend acknowledging the loss and the stress of being an executor. The letter should be reflective of you and your style but focused on the recipient. That is, if you are very formal, your letter should reflect that.

However, if your style is more casual and laidback, it is alright to reflect that too. You do not want to present something that you are not in your mailings. Your message should reflect that you are here to help during this difficult time. Highlight that you can make the selling of a house easy, fast, and painless.

- **Have A Conversation with The Executor** - ideally, the executor will initiate the phone call after receiving your mailer. However, if you are not getting return calls, you may want to make phone calls yourself. The key to these calls is to be prepared to listen. You will want to let the executor do of the talking and only guide the conversation with your questions. Many executors are in a particularly tough time in their life, and they need someone to talk to. If you can listen, you are providing something the executor needs, and you are on your way to developing the rapport that will be necessary to move this potential transaction forward.

- **Build That Relationship with The Executor** - understand the unique situation of the executor and determine if you can help in any way. Often the executor does not live near the house. Offering to run by and check on the house, pick up the newspaper, or even mow the yard can be a huge help to the executor.
Once you have built a rapport with the Executor, you are well on your way to determining if this property is of interest to you, and you can proceed as you would with any other opportunity.

- **Persistence is Key** - in the scenario outlined above, you have contacted the executor and can build a relationship. It takes time and persistence to be in this position. You will not receive a call from many of your leads. They simply are not interested in your help for a variety of reasons. However, if you continue to work the leads and are continually adding new leads to your pipeline, you will have success.

Having access to leads on a regular basis means that you will be able to success in probate real estate investing. With time, patience, and a carefully thought-out business plan, you can be confident that time will make an enormous difference in your ability to purchase homes and other properties at a favorable price. Here again, the key to success is reaching out to executors. This allows you time to work probates and to patiently await those executors who do not want to sell immediately.

Lead Generation Categories:

Offline Lead Generation Methods - this is anything that does not involve the internet. Direct mail, newspaper classifieds, referrals and networking, door hangers, etc. Mostly off-line lead generation can be considered outbound marketing.

Online Lead Generation Methods - if properly employed, these methods can be incredibly cost effective and scalable. This is anything that takes place on the internet:

- Google AdWords and local business listings.
- Social media marketing.
- Craigslist and similar sites

Hybrid - marketing methods using both online and offline lead generation in some form. For example:

- Sending a postcard to someone directing them to go to your website and fill out a form (this can be a buyer or a seller).

- Posting your phone number on your website directing potential sellers to call you instead of having them fill out a form.

Making an Offer on Probate Properties
Before you make an offer on a probate property, do your research. Understand what must be paid to clear the property (i.e., mortgage, back taxes, past due utilities, or other liens on the property). All probate properties are not lien free.

Once your offer is accepted by the estate's representative, the court must approve the sale. This process could take 30 to 45 days (or even longer) before approval. So, be prepared for time-consuming court proceedings. If you are patient (and prepared) you can land a great deal on the home.

THE INSPECTION

Visiting the Property
Arrive at the property promptly at the scheduled time. As you go through the house with the seller you should ask them if they are aware of any specific problems with the house. In doing so, you gain information about the condition of the house, but more importantly you are positioning yourself for negotiation. Additionally, by noticing and mentioning problem areas you are subtly devaluing the house.

All sellers think their house is in better condition than it really is. When you point things out as you go along you are quietly presenting the true condition.

The Numbers
At this point you have taken the tour, built rapport, noticed all the repair items and taken plenty of pictures (with their permission of course). Now it is time to talk numbers.

- NEVER make an offer on the spot!
- Before you leave ask the Seller "If I pay cash, and buy the house, 'as-is,' what is the bottom-line price to get this deal done?"

Expect a lower number than they told you on the phone. Sellers often come down to reality after you point out repair items throughout the house. Sometimes people say, "I don't know, make me an offer." The truth is that they have a number in mind, but they are unsure as to whether the number they are thinking is realistic or not.

Negotiating Strategy
Always refer to your partner - you always want to present yourself as though you must check EVERYTHING with a partner (even if it just YOU). This allows you to get the seller to agree to something, like the price, but allows you to still go back and talk to your partner. When you are negotiating, avoid the trap of wanting to be the decision maker in the eyes of the seller.

You want to take the time to calculate the offer. Give yourself the time to evaluate the ARV, your photos, and your repair estimate. You get this time by letting the Seller know that you need to discuss the deal with your partner.

The Offer

Making the Offer consists of the following steps:

- Determine the After Repaired Value (ARV).
- Estimate the renovations necessary to bring the house to marketable condition.
- Calculate the offer depending on whether the house is in a buy and hold neighborhood or flip neighborhood.
- Present the offer to the Seller.
- Follow-up until the DEAL is SETTLED.

Calculate the following two numbers before speaking to the owner:

- Starting offer price.
- Maximum offer price.

Never, never make an offer over the phone. Do it in person, so set-up the appointment. When negotiating with the seller, say **"I have good news, my partner and I decided to make an offer. We can pay cash, close the deal within 30 days, and buy the house "as-is." The offer is XXX thousand dollars." THEN SHUT UP!**

The Seller may flat out tell you that that number does not work. Ask them, **"What REALISTIC number do you have in mind that DOES work?"**

If they say a number back that WILL GET THE DEAL DONE for THEM, you say, **"I do not know if I could do that number, but if I could get my partner to agree at that price, DO WE HAVE A DEAL?"**

THE AGREEMENT

A Signed Agreement of Sale is an ASSET! Without a signed agreement, you have nothing.

How to Prepare the Agreement

Important items to include in your Purchase Agreement are:

1. Seller's full name, if more than one person all names must be shown. If all the names on deed are deceased and you are buying the property from the heirs, put "The Estate of [the last living owner's name]" as the Seller.
2. Replace your name or company name as the Buyer.
3. Insert the entire address in the legal description.
4. Insert the parcel or tax ID number.
5. Purchase price is the total purchase price.
6. Cash deposit amount which you should deposit at the title company or closing agent who will handle your settlement.
7. How much do you put as the cash deposit? You put down as little as possible, but not more than $500.

Remember, the purchase price must always be approved by the court!

Always Sign in Person
If possible, GO SIGN THE AGREEMENT IN PERSON. Many Sellers will tell you to send over the agreement so that they can look at it. No way! Ask them again, "Do we have a deal?" Insist on meeting them in person to go over the agreement together.

How to Sign the Agreement with the Seller
When you meet with the Seller to go over the paperwork remember that your goal is to GET THE AGREEMENT SIGNED. (Print 2 copies before you go to meet them, you give one copy to them, and keep the other).

Only Cover the Important Items

You are not the Sellers' attorney or real estate agent! It is not your job to go over every detail of the agreement, you cover the few sections that have important information TO YOU. You can:

- Point out the Sellers & Buyers names and ask if the spelling is correct.

- Point out the address and ask if it appears correctly.

- Point out the sale price and deposit amounts.

- Show them the acceptance date, which is usually that day's date.

- Point out the closing date; and if they ask why it takes so long (usually 35 days out), title report may take 2 weeks, and that there may be documents necessary to clear that title report.

You can also tell them that you often close your deals ahead of the scheduled settlement date but want to make sure there is plenty of time to clear title. Most sellers have no problem with this. In the real estate world, 30 to 35-day closings are FAST.

Resume your explanation and ask if there is any litigation pending that you need to know about, such as foreclosure, divorce, bankruptcy, etc.

LETTER TO THE ESTATE EXECUTOR | ADMINISTRATOR

Dear <   >

I would like to take this opportunity to introduce myself and my company **'Probate Property Helper.'** My name is<   >, and I help people like yourself who have inherited real property.

At Probate Property Helper, we work hard to take the pressure out of dealing with a deceased loved one's estate. No matter if you are unable to deal with the financial commitments of maintaining the property or you are looking for a quick sale, we are here to guide you through the property buying process. We purchase inherited homes quickly, discreetly, and ethically often exchanging contracts in under 48 hours. Every year we purchase dozens of inherited properties based upon referrals, our reputation and word of mouth.

Our team understands the stress of handling the sale of a family member's estate and will work with you in a sensitive and transparent manner throughout the process. We purchase homes directly through executors and beneficiaries, cutting out the middlemen and save you money in the process.

Why Sell A House to Probate Property Helper?
While there are other ways to sell your property, relying on Probate Property Helper makes sense. We take out the time, cost and pressures involved in the sale of an inherited home. What is more, our service is completely free to use, and we guarantee to make an offer on the home, regardless of its location or condition. In using Probate Property Helper there is no need to prepare the property for marketing, maintenance, or house clearance. We buy properties in any condition, even if they are un-mortgageable. There are no real estate agent's fees to pay and we can even cover your legal fees.

Get in touch with us today for a free property purchase estimation.

AFTERWORD

Thank you for reading

PROBATE
A Complete Guide for Real Estate Investors

We hope you enjoyed this Real Estate Knowledge Publication

Thank you again valued reader,
and we hope to meet you again on another book.

ABOUT THE AUTHOR

Pierre Mouchette is the Founder and CEO of Real Property Experts LLC. He is a graduate of New York University, with a Master's in Business Administration, a Certificate in Real Estate Law - Fairfield University - CT, Graduate of the Realtors Institute – CT, and held licensing as a Real Estate Broker, and a Mortgage Broker.

Pierre is currently authoring Books, Booklets, How-to-Articles, and Guides in retirement. Pierre has an extensive background in real estate investment, business management and sales, supplemented by decades of hands-on-experience in building systems engineering, development, evaluation, and assorted analytical engineering studies.

Using background knowledge and experience, Pierre launched Real Property Experts in 2013 to help simplify real estate investing by connecting investors through innovative technology. In 2018, Pierre created THE SYNCHRONICITY INVESTOR a real estate website to facilitate providing world-class solutions for real estate investors and investment businesses.

Real Estate Knowledge Publications

By Pierre Mouchette

VALUE ADDED STRATEGIES

ASSET INVESTOR

PROBATE - A Complete Guide for Real Estate Investors

Protecting Your Assets in The Pandemic Age

Creating An Itemized Asset List

The Methodology of Finding Inventory for Jobbers and Wholesalers

The Real Estate Investors Ladder to Success

The Methodology of Finding Distressed Properties for Bird-Dogs

How to Create A List Buyers

The Dynamics of a Real Estate Wholesaler

Numbers for Wholesalers

Getting Started in Real Estate Investing as A Hacker

How To Become a Real Estate LOCATOR or BIRD-DOG

The Ultimate Guide to Starting Your Own Business

PASSIVE INVESTING

Passive Real Estate Investing

Passive Investing Thru Real Estate Investment Trusts

www.ingramcontent.com/pod-product-compliance
Lightning Source LLC
Chambersburg PA
CBHW081658220526
45466CB00009B/2804